A HEART STIRRED FOR FELLOWSHIP

AN UNFINISHED STORY

PENNED BY DON STIVER

Copyright © 2024 Penned By Don Stiver

All rights reserved.

No part of this book may be reproduced in any form or by any electronic or mechanical means, including information storage and retrieval systems, without written permission from the author, except for the use of brief quotations in a book review.

"Scripture quotations taken from the (NASB®) New American Standard Bible®, Copyright © 1960, 1971, 1977, 1995, by The Lockman Foundation. Used by permission. All rights reserved. lockman.org"

Scripture quotations from THE MESSAGE REMIX. Copyright © by Eugene H. Peterson 1993, 2002, 2005, 2018. Used by permission of NavPress. All rights reserved. Represented by Tyndale House Publishers, Inc.

Cover Design by John Bryll Pulido; website : brilliantcover.com

Formatted by Ruth L. Snyder

1st Edition Paperback (B & W): 978-1-7382403-8-8

2nd Edition Paperback (Color): 978-1-998542-03-1

Ebook: 978-1-7382403-9-5

CONTENTS

Acknowledgments	v
Introduction	ix
1. Dreams and Visions	1
2. From Woodstock to the Slammer	7
3. I Learned a Lot in Prison	13
4. Sweeney, Now There's a Good Irish Name	17
5. I See That Hand!	21
6. What Would Moses Do?	25
7. Closure: By Susan Stiver	29
About the Author	31

ACKNOWLEDGMENTS

This book was written by a man who loved and sought God
with all his heart while here in this earthly realm.
Now he continues to love and spend time with his Creator
in the Heavenlies.

God stirred his heart for fellowship here,
and taught him how to see and love people
as God sees and loves them.

He never knew a stranger,
and he so wanted everyone
to know, and be known,
by their Creator, God.

Then, and only then,
will there be true love, unity,
And fellowship
as it is meant to be.

May you hear God's heart for you as Don shares his journey,
and the revelations given to him by our Father, God.
Then allow God to finish the book in you.

DEDICATION

*This book is dedicated with love to
all of our children and grandchildren.*

*So teach us to number our days,
That we may present to You
a heart of wisdom.*

*Psalm 90:12
(New American Standard Bible 1995)*

INTRODUCTION

"There's a book in you," I was told one day as I traveled across Ireland with a diverse team of ministers. We were about twenty-five in number, from various parts of the world. I had never given a moment's thought of such a suggestion in my entire lifetime, but I was willing to receive this word from the prophetess as she singled me out on our tour bus. The company was traveling together seeing the sights of Ireland after participating in a Prophetic Conference in Bray, Ireland the week before. Fellowship was "over-the-top" great as we traveled together and got to know one another on this week's tour. My thoughts: "Why couldn't it be like this more often? Fellowship among like believers, and all of us having just witnessed God doing great restorative work in Ireland." My love for God's people began to take on a greater depth.

About one and a half years prior [to this trip], having known and heard a prophet of our time, Bob Jones, relate his story of going to Heaven, and being asked the question, "Did you learn to love?", I found myself contemplating these words.

I consider myself an intercessor, and I love the life of intercession. I will go into depth on this later, but for now, I found I lacked a lot in the love department. I began asking The Lord for help because I knew I needed it. After all, I have to drive in city traffic, and on our interstates, and hear the news. My main thrust of intercession at the time was for this nation. I learned so much and was drawn so very close to the heart of God, but I had this little sub-prayer back there – love.

[Then in] September 2019, just prior to departure for Ireland, The Lord abruptly stopped my focus for this nation and instructed me to begin praising Him for the things that are forthcoming. This transition was quite difficult for me, from the trenches to the praise band. I had learned weaponry, not instruments. Oh, but God has a way with things, and I love to go new places.

[In December 2019] Sue and I attended a New Years Conference at MorningStar, Fort Mill, SC, where we were guests at a dear friend and sister-in-Christ's writing room. I think it was a set-up! Instead of sleep that night, The Lord took me on a trip of visions/dreams, and the most delightful experiences I can remember.

CHAPTER 1
DREAMS AND VISIONS

I love the times we live in as we step into the fulfillment of so many Bible prophecies, such as Joel's foretelling of dreams and visions, which was reinforced by Peter in his rendering of Pentecost. This became the case in my life, and now in this room while attempting to sleep. The Lord had things He wanted to show me.

Sue and I had recently purchased a book by Anna Roundtree, (two in one actually), where she gives her account of a trip (all expenses paid) into Heaven. We intended to read it soon after the New Year, and we had left it at home. I have also read Rick Joyner's account of trips into Heaven, and loved to learn of such experiences. Paul, Daniel, John, and others have had experiences much like Isaiah, where seeing into Heaven becomes their reality! What I didn't know about Anna's book is that it would become a sort of confirmation to the things I would see the first night of the Conference.

Sue and I were so tired, and we turned in early, after a very long day beginning at 4:30am. I have tried to give a detailed account of the dreams and visions of that night, but it was much like watching the most wonderful three ring circus imaginable. I was seeing what was shown, yet perceiving more than the seeing. The Lord brought people in front of me and I saw them in, it's hard to explain, but shades of joy and colors so expressive tied to their nature. Revelation of these things flooded the room for example. Romans 14:17 tells us: "The Kingdom of God is not food and drink, but righteousness and peace and joy in the Holy Spirit." So, can you imagine joy being the color yellow? Imagine righteousness the color red, and peace blue; the primary colors. Now think of people you know who are joyful, or have great peace, or are strong in righteousness. These things belong to us as Christ's people, and should all abide in us as we abide in Him, but what I was seeing that night was God's people parading before me exploding with such vivid color and joyfulness, and love seemed to be everywhere. It was hard to contain. I enjoyed this display for about three hours while my wife slept soundly. I found myself in such a joyful, fun place, it had me bursting with pure joy – almost like you could swim in it. I expressed to The Lord I might need to do the same as Sue, and sleep, so He gave me a break around 11pm. I drifted off to sleep, finally!

3:00am my eyes popped wide open, and we were off again. Somehow, I was rested, and now very excited. I began understanding what The Lord was showing me, which are several things.

The people were as He sees them; completed works and in glorified state. He showed me His Kingdom people in a place that is for us now. Let me say I was seeing in The Spirit; however, we live in this physical realm. The Lord impressed upon me He is intending to bring His Kingdom to this earth very soon, but this comes with, shall I say, instructions.

I had read Psalm 45 a few days earlier, and I questioned The Lord at that time as I read it. He "invited me inside" the palace as this flurry of activity took place in this Bridal Preparation Psalm.

THE PRELUDE TO MY NIGHT OF VISIONS.

What The Lord was emphasizing is that these are nobility, royalty, all members and honored guests, and the jubilance is tangible in this place. The Lord made it very plain to me He is about to answer so many prayers – Your Kingdom come, Your will be done – and we are moving into the actual preparation time. Oh, be assured it is for all, but pay close attention to the instructions.

I think the opportunity is coming quickly, but the actual time of completion will seem like forever to us. Opportunity: when Jesus finished the Beatitudes, and His teaching on the mountain, He headed down and did some healing, marveled at the centurion's faith, and demonstrated His place and power, but He was on the move. A scribe and a disciple came to Him, and wanted to know what signing up with Him might be like. We are not told their outcome, but we do know Jesus didn't paint them a rosy picture; rather militant, if I say so myself. And then the ship sailed, much like the door closing after the five wise virgins trimmed their lamps and followed the Bridegroom.

I eventually went back to sleep after this segment of the vision; there is more to be explained later. I had a dream just before wakening. A couple I knew in my past, who married around fifty plus years ago, were standing before me, dressed to the hilt and beaming. I approached them thinking how beautiful they looked, and intended to greet the man first, but the lady extended her white-gloved hand for my greeting. I took her hand, and the dream ended. I asked a very trusted brother, a dream interpreter, for his thoughts, and my heart bore great witness to his explanation. The lady, my school "buddy" and the first girl I ever kissed, once I thought girls weren't covered with cooties, was a type of "first love"; her spouse is a picture of wholeness. You should have seen his outfit! The Interpretation:

First Love and Wholeness walk together, but your first love must be embraced first, and wholeness will accompany her as one.

Going back to my night of visions, this was understood in a different way. But this dream emphasized it. The vision of The Lord's Kingdom coming down was so beautiful, whole and joyous. I knew as we began to see God's people as He sees them, we would step into a new level of understanding, or discerning The Lord's body – the church – which would result in the wholeness and well-being we strive for, but so seldom fully obtain. When we enter this place of Kingdom love and sight, we will operate in a spiritual level we know exists, but we seldom reach.

The rest of this book will be an attempt at trying to explain why we try so hard and still fall short. Jesus was able to heal everybody. Why can't we? Why do we pray and watch those close to us still die? I'm not sure The Lord showed me everything, but I am excited with what He did show me.

Most everything we obtain seems to last for a season, and the understanding is not fully understood, as in healing. So often a healing, or prophetic word will be delivered with a dose of spookiness to the receiver, and the Kingdom of God stays somewhat beyond our reach or comprehension.

I'd like to go ahead and just get the devil out of the way. So let's look at his part and get done with him. As I wrote, I saw God's people, people I love dearly, in a light only God could reveal to me – Kingdom Light, if you will. Why don't we see each other that way all of the time? Aren't our eyes of understanding open; don't we see spiritually? Why are many sick, weak, afflicted, and even asleep? After all, aren't we also made in the image and likeness of God? Now who do we imagine would just delight in marring or defaming that image? That would be Satan. If he can walk you through the stockyards, you will come out with stink and manure on your boots, especially if he shoves you down while you're there. What about running you into briars or sandspurs, are you huggable with spurs all over you? Any analogy could be made for the unattractive appearance we have as a result of walking through this world. It gets worse, but please remember Jesus is offering us an opportunity, and the ship will sail!

I prayed long and hard with what I am about to suggest because it is The Bride of Christ that I am going to be examining for the bulk of the remainder of this book. We must ask ourselves, are we a bride prepared without spot or wrinkle? The next chapters will be crude, but honest. They may be general, and each one [of us] will have to do some self-examination, but it will be healthy. I am certain the religious spirit will rise up against the following, and especially me, but I am determined to follow Jesus, so let's go. I am willing because love is behind it all.

CHAPTER 2
FROM WOODSTOCK TO THE SLAMMER

Just for the record, I did not go to Woodstock. There were multiple Pop Festivals during that time, and I attended others. I just didn't hit the "Biggy". But now the Slammer is another subject!

People got naked at Woodstock. Have you ever been arrested and done any time? First thing you experience is they strip you naked and you start from there. Jesus experienced this, and it is humiliating. I think everybody should spend at least ten days in at least jail. There is a difference between jail and prison, but the sound of the door slamming is identical. Incarceration, wow that sounds almost squeaky clean, and can mean an arrest for suspicion, or serving a life sentence. But incarceration is an institution and minister of God.

There is so much to learn, but let me return to Woodstock, or rather the thing that brought on the "Jesus Movement", the Hippie days. How do you view it? Was it The Lord, or was it the Devil? Remember, many people didn't recognize Jesus when He came the first time. I wouldn't even try to say it was The Lord, but I still say, having lived through all of that, that The Lord was right there in the midst. He indeed will never leave us or forsake us. I also have to say, the traditional church was looking somewhere else for the most part.

The Scriptures tell the story of Jesus walking through Israel, and encountering all of mankind – movers and shakers, poor and needy, seekers and believers, freeloaders and the arrogant. As He engaged them, He would try to bring them back to square one, much like the institution of prison will do to a person. Jesus would point to where to start, but many were unable to see Him. Fortunately, many did see Him and listened. For them, the cell door opened. The others got comfortable in their environment and defended it; justified who they were and what they did, much like prison life.

[Jesus said] "Love the Lord God with all your heart, and with all your soul, and with all your mind." His words were bathed in love; a good medicine. It's like "Here's your sign!". But He didn't leave it there, He went on to tell them to love one another like you love yourselves. But they only sought to bring Him in line. He was pointing to life abundant. They saw someone who simply wouldn't line up with their thinking. In my chapter "I See That Hand", what we do today is what was done to Him two thousand years ago. If someone is Spirit-filled and burning for God, usually that one needs to be brought into line. Who do they think they are? And let's check their credentials. This is how we do church.

Raised Catholic by parents who "knew the rules" but were like everyone else in that situation; they didn't know Latin [incomplete thought, but it sets the stage].

∼

I was raised in Central Florida back when it was still paradise – pre-Disney. We lived close to the St John's River, about 25 miles east of Orlando. The Catholic Church we attended was called a Mission Church. We met, at first recollection, at a pavilion on a lake. Typical for Florida, it was a screened in pavilion on the grounds around a lake. Well for a young boy, this was great! All I had to do was keep quiet while some spooky guy would show up, always in a hurry, and put on a really fancy white cape (capes are so cool) over his black tight-fitting dress, and go up front and mumble a bunch of words in a foreign language. I could look outside and daydream, and there were plenty of woods around to hold my interest.

When the service was over, we wouldn't ever discuss what all that was about. We just knew to show up and then not to break the long list of rules. On that subject, my position in this family made it easy for me. There were no great expectations on me; not the first born, not the only girl child, and not the youngest. So as the middle boy, it was easy to avoid ever being noticed. I learned that to break a rule had to be something major, and I seldom did that, thus enjoying my stealth position in the family. I believed in God, as did all good Catholics, and I lived life thinking I was covered by association. The problem with that was there seemed to be no association with others of the same faith. You were trained to make note of who else might be Catholic and told to steer clear of those who aren't. Romans 16:17 tells you to do just that. Could it be that was the basis of the separation between the Catholic faith and protestants? Sure, anyone can go back to Martin Luther and make strong argument for the factions, but on a simple person's life, how can you criticize someone keeping distance if they are warned or perceive a danger as Paul guided those he wrote to?

My mother, the youngest of eleven, was born in 1920. She had two siblings born in the late 1800's. I have sought The Lord for answers concerning fellowship, unity, love, and many other Christian virtues. One day The Lord showed me some differences. As an infant, Mamma could likely lay in a playpen in her backyard and see a Model T ride by, an airplane fly overhead, and hear a radio play in her hearing range. Her older siblings, as infants, would experience none of the above. Same parents, same family, but completely different points of reference. It's the same with each generation, but people tend to look for differences, not common unity. It seems society busies themselves with their own lives and reserves that task [of unity] for the government. While government dilutes everything, sizes it to fit the slowest, laziest, weakest among us, and government feels it has done well. But good parents examine their children and early on encourages them to head in the direction they are prone to travel.

Romans 16:17 encourages distance from those who stand apart, those of disunity, and for good reason. We need time to see and understand others and they need the same. It is so important to learn in life to listen to God's Holy Spirit, and be led by Him rather than a crowd follower who goes through life thinking they are fine. They are covered, after all.

Jesus certainly was, to the rest of the world, one who stood apart. Some loved that about Him, most hated it, and by in large, that is what got Him killed. His teaching attempted to give explanation to life, but "the club" was quite comfortable with business as usual – no room for dissension.

But now, I was on my way to Woodstock or the Slammer, right? So, Jesus offered explanations of life – life abundant. The first Book of Corinthians tells us in Chapter 1, verse 21, that man's thinking never brought mankind into fellowship with God. What I love about prison is you don't have a lot to stand on, and you know your own thinking got you in there, so you're in a position of looking for answers. A long with that, often God will give to those who are indeed looking, a level of discernment. Most inmates can read a person in a matter of seconds. Prophetic? Street wise? Experienced? We know The Lord watches over all His creation, and desires the best for us. He is God-of-second-chances, and gives generously. Why would He not give discernment to those who so need it at this time in their life? Everyone incarcerated is looking for a way out – some honestly; others continue leaning on their own understanding, and thinking themselves wise, will try to work an angle. The gifts of God are without repentance, so the discerning can be used to "get over" on another human being. But, now we are beginning to drift into politics, and we haven't yet gone to Woodstock.

CHAPTER 3
I LEARNED A LOT IN PRISON

Those who know me well know that sooner or later, I will bring the conversation around to prison. The best years of my life were spent there. Also, I think one of my very best friends, and one who influenced me a lot, I met in prison. He died a few years back, and I miss him very much, but we will meet again. When The Lord graciously saved me, I was on a path that most likely would have resulted in a good long stay behind bars. But God had other plans for me. I'm glad He is Lord!

When I gave my heart to Jesus, I almost immediately understood I belonged in prison. A Spirit-filled believer led me to The Lord and pointed toward a Spirit-filled life. God was talking to me about it. I think the jury may have still been out concerning me. Either that or The Lord was just having some real fun with me.

I came to Jesus at the last days or few years of the Jesus Movement. I was a hippie, living somewhat on the road, and hitchhiking across southern Virginia. A very prophetic man [gave me a ride], presented the gospel to me with a word from The Lord to return to Florida, my childhood home. I took a job with an Electrical Construction Company, and was sent to Cross City Florida to build a prison. I stayed in a motel where I prayed, read the Word, smoked a joint, played the guitar, and then would repeat in no particular order. Oh, I played mostly Christian songs. Those days were filled with revelations, and sweet, sweet times with The Lord. I went through deliverance, and was freed from so many vices. Just me and The Lord in Cross City – heaven on earth. As an ex-hippie, I didn't know a lot, especially about church. I kept reading in God's Word about fellowship, and The Holy Spirit was drawing me. "Fellowship" is the very word The Lord used to bring me into church back in 1977. I was raised out in the country as a young Catholic back in the Latin speaking days. I knew very little about God, or church, or life. I did know that I didn't care for religion, and knew how to recognize it. My last Catholic service I attended was at age 17, so I drifted for the next eight years hoping not to get drafted, or busted, during those "Hippie" days, and the Vietnam Conflict (War).

Now I found a job and a prison to build. I hired an inmate from the facility to be my helper. He was a paper hanger. Hopefully the reader realizes here that a paper hanger is a confidence "Con" man, who does his crime with paper, i.e. bad checks, fraud, forgery, etc. Nice guy, very likable, and a pretty good worker. He spun me a very convincing tale about how his drafting instructor would so much appreciate a set of real drawings like we used, and arranged for me to send a set to the facility via him. Yes, I fell for it. Fortunately, a few days later his cell block was busted pouring over the points highlighting the weak points. Told you I didn't know a lot!

Well, another Bible word I was learning was "discernment", and oh how I needed it. I prayed for discernment, and I did receive a good portion, but I learned it could be a blessing or a curse at times. For me, as I learned more and used this gift, I also learned if it is used without great measures of love, it can destroy someone. Guilty as charged.

∽

As stated, by now it was late 1977, and I had been a Christian for a year and a half.

Drawn by the word "fellowship", I was now in my first church, complete with another new word, "baptism". The days were so alive, and fellowship was sweet. The revelations and insights into God's Word just kept coming. The pastors of this very small fellowship encouraged me to enroll in Bible College. The husband was a Georgia native, and salvation's message was his mode of operation. His wife traveled with Aimee Semple McPherson as a young lady, and was apt in the gifts of The Spirit; a great place to be. They had love for everyone, and times were good. My willingness to serve, and relationship with The Lord placed me on the rise in that fellowship only to cause great levels of jealousy from some who had been there much longer than myself. A very odd predicament for one who loves The Lord, desires to serve, and was willing to serve in any way. I was learning remember, church was all brand new to me. I also got my eyes opened to how messed up and wounded people are – work to do.

While attending International Seminary in Orlando, Florida, some other brothers made it known they were involved in prison ministry. My heart leapt! These brothers took me on as one of them, but my home church had me wearing about five other hats – Associate Pastor, Youth Director, Sunday School Superintendent, Usher, and Building Committee member. A formula for burnout – and burnout I did. Sadly, prison ministry took a back burner to it all, and as one can guess – things got worse. The husband-and-wife team were stretched too thin as well, and we were in a building project at the time. Ultimately, they turned the fellowship over to the Assemblies of God. It came as a huge surprise to me that although my degree was accredited, AG didn't recognize it. Some new things to learn about how the Body of Christ functions. I was thinking "all in one accord".

I'm giving a fair rendering of my life, and walk, but only for the purpose of relating to Jesus' wonderful Bride, The Church. I had had a vision a few years earlier, at the time of my baptism, that showed me the next twenty years of my life. Salvation was an absolute "Road to Damascus" experience; total darkness to full light, and alive for the first time. Assuming baptism would be as dynamic, or spectacular was the wrong assumption. We had a lake in the center of our small town. Our fellowship used that lake for this baptism occasion. The whole community hung out there on Sunday afternoon, and down I went. The following week was spent inquiring of The Lord if something was wrong, or incomplete. The answer came in an open vision the following Sunday during worship. It began in a body of water where I rose up to the surface. It was so wonderful – like paradise. A doe came and drank from the water, and as she did, I was drawn up over her head. She lifted her head and took a few steps, then stopped and looked back at the pool. Two fawns walked up behind her, then she walked into the dark forest up the hill as [the vision] ended.

A few months later, during a fast, and at the beginning of my burning out phase, I was called upon to fix some electrical problems at a girl's house. As I finished and she offered me some water, I heard very plainly a voice that said, "This is the doe". Let me just say here, I made an assumption and did not have, or take the time to seek The Lord. We married and had two children. Let's see now… where did I leave that discernment?

But this chapter is about things learned in prison, right? The trips I took to Florida State Prison were great! Good fellowship, as several of us traveled the distance one and a half hour each way. We served at the East Unit. There are six facilities on that property, a receiving medical center, "O" Unit which is support – like cutting the grass, and garbage disposal. The one we went to is where "Sparky", the electric chair, and the Death Row inmates are housed. I had had visions and dreams already [unfinished sentence and thought]

CHAPTER 4
SWEENEY, NOW THERE'S A GOOD IRISH NAME

Well, it is! I'm going to borrow the name for the sake of this chapter. Hopefully all Sweeneys are okay with that. After all, the Irish are indeed fun-loving people.

Jesus taught us a few things we trip all over. I've been a Christian for almost 44 years at this time, and I cannot recall ever hearing Matthew 23:6-10 preached on. That's the chapter where Jesus exposes the leaders of His time, and even goes into some very real detail.

> "They love the places of honor at banquets and the chief seats in the synagogues, and respectful greetings in the market places, and being called Rabbi by men. But do not be called Rabbi; for One is your Teacher, and you are all brothers. Do not call anyone on earth your father; for One is your Father, He who is in heaven. Do not be called leaders; for One is your Leader, that is Christ." (NASB1995)

But now what does any of this have to do with poor Sweeney?

When I finished Bible College in the late 70's, and now had a few letters to add to my name – along with the prefix – it took some adjustment. Is this what The Lord meant about doors opening? I mean, wow, you play the Reverand card and people step back and let you come on in; hospitals, community centers, special events, even the better business association wants your endorsement.

I was brand new to all this, and a very slow learner as well. I wasn't raised in a Protestant Church where English was spoken, so I was way behind. I heard a lot in Seminary, just didn't have a lot of reference points, but then there was this love of adventure.

Upon ordination, I knew I was not to, as everyone asked me, "take a church". Rather The Lord told me, "Son, you belong in prison." God never lies! My job at the time was electrical construction in Central Florida during the long-lasting Disney Boom. The electricians "go by" book is the National Electrical Code. They cost a good bit, so if you leave one on your other things and it's not nailed down, it can walk. The name on the inside cover of mine read: Rev. Don Stiver. I left off the extra letters after my name. All this, and it was still just as gone as that first piece of bacon in the kitchen before it hits the table.

Sweeney, the Irishman, worked for me on one of my construction jobs. He was a character – wide open and unfiltered. He would have run the world if people would just listen to him. He could also be a bit contrary, but I love a challenge. We had our dynamics until one day he brought me my code book with a question, "Is this yours? I found it somewhere." I thanked him, and then I noticed everything changed on that job site. Not only did Sweeney cease to be Sweeney, others changed as well. It sucked, these guys were fun and real, but now they were cautious and guarded.

Now let's look at Matthew 23 again. These words are two thousand years old, so we have had all of this time to get it right. But the problems have multiplied, not decreased. Honor is a very good thing, but I have watched many go to extremes in order to obtain the praises of men. Could it be our titles and letters surrounding our name are spots, wrinkles, blemishes, or outright stench? And what about poor Sweeney? What made him so paralyzed when I was around from that day on? Jesus was telling us where to focus. He really made it quite simple; we are all brothers, eliminating titles. Your Father is in heaven, focus on and follow Jesus, your Leader, The Word of God.

So, what's the problem? There's a catch, surely. Have you ever heard someone put some bass in their voice and switch over to seventeenth century English when they address "Gawd"? Yes, you have. How about professional theatrics like dropping prostate on the floor before a select little group of disciples? Now that's impressive, so humble. They'd never try that in public though. Blingy clothes, gold chains, and poser pants – you know, [the jeans bought with holes]; not really worn out. I've actually known for a fact that the opening statement of a highly favored friend of a prominent Fellowship's Founder, was a bold face lie. The man preached on and people wowed him, but he lost me with the lie. Why would someone do such a thing? It's because we are all men, and we love the praise of men. Jesus tried to steer us away from such practices, but we are so slow to learn. It's easy enough for today's clergy to point and say, "Yeah, those Pharisees were really a mess, why they even crucified Jesus." Well, they were just the clergy of Jesus' time, and the word synagogue was simply their fellowship buildings. No news here.

Okay, and the Sweeneys drive all of this because the bling, theatrics, wise words and smooth talk impress them. They, like everyone else, look horizonal instead of where Jesus pointed. What do we see when we look about? Sweeney sees me as a man of the cloth; my wrinkle or blemish. Why? The chump in the corner, Satan, has placed a set of glasses on Sweeney so he sees through them. Now instead of seeing me as one of God's unique creations, full of treasure and life, he sees restrictions instead of the words of life, a snitch instead of righteousness. It goes on, he may see his own inadequacies; that's one the devil loves to use. Sweeney needs to look up, then he couldn't see me.

Have you ever heard the term "sheep bites"? I know things happen in churches. The stories I've heard at the places I've been could equal a set of Brittanicas. Pastors get to the point where they are so beat down, and the chump laughs on. Could it be that the enemy puts a set of his glasses on [them] that makes others appear inconsiderate, selfish, unwilling to help or show compassion, too needy, or critical? Those glasses can filter out God's beauty, and actually highlight some of the spots and wrinkles God is in the process of eliminating. Pastors pour a lot into people and hope for, or expect a little something in return. Big wide difference between "hope for" and "expect". When you hire someone, you should "expect"; when you serve, you "hope". When you start looking at all your sheep bites, well maybe we should be looking at the Author and Finisher of our faith, which is so precious in God's sight. Remember, He carried more than a few.

CHAPTER 5
I SEE THAT HAND!

I have sat in so many fellowship meetings where the question was asked, "How many here have been hurt or wounded in church?" Hands up everywhere. People leave church for dozens of reasons. Usually everyone from the top down has an opinion as to why, and most are more than willing to share – right or wrong. The fact is harmony is, shall we say, interrupted. I love harmony. I used to sing melody in a gospel band some years back. Good harmony is fun and pleasant; probably has a color like rich emerald green or something. I think about a youthful young lady with locks of curly red hair and an emerald green dress, singing like a song bird. But when she's missing…………

The reasons people leave are many, and they should be looked at rather than discounted. In the Bible belt, we have churches of the same denomination a block or two apart, and they are not outreach churches. They are the result of church splits. Where did Harmony wind up going? Well, that depends on the strength of her glasses, or the glasses the next fellowship prefers. It's hard to lay down a set of glasses once you've gotten used to them.

. . .

My years of Christianity have taken me to eight different fellowships. Now in all fairness, this includes a move across several states. Point is, there are a number of examples to be drawn from firsthand.

In my "view" (glasses), it broke down like this. In the first fellowship, I experienced jealousy from fellow believers. It was a small church and others were firmly in place prior to my arrival. I was very close to The Lord, and this "Jesus Freak" as we were called, upset the apple cart. It got rough, but God is faithful. That fellowship turned the reigns over to a denominational fellowship. The new pastor wanted to start fresh. I was part of the old guard, and he made it very clear there was not room for me. I went to the next town [which was] much larger, and attended a major denomination's large facility. I watched for about two years while the congregation gave the very sweet, humble pastor the boot. He thought their growth problems needed to spread out; the community wanted to build a mega church.

I moved several states away and found sweet fellowship in a small country church. Then I went through a divorce. Another chapter perhaps. Bottom line here, I moved to the other side of the county, and attended [yet another] major denominational church. I suppose you could say I went out of the frying pan into the fire. My Christian life [had been] on hold for a very long time up until now, but once again the dreams, visions, and revelations were back, and I was so very happy. But the pastor at the major denomination wasn't so much so. He didn't believe in the gifts of The Spirit, and had a hard time being around them. I was viewed as one who wears the enemy's colors; once again top-down persecution. That makes two times. The stay lasted about four years. During that time, I met Sue. We loved that fellowship, but there was such an atmosphere of question, [and misunderstanding].

∼

The Spirit of God then lead Sue and I to an old denomination. We were warmly welcomed. The pastor was Spirit-filled and full of life. We became great friends. However, the governing board of that church wasn't on the same page as the pastor and his wife. We stuck close to them through mediation. He too, like other pastors we had seen, got the boot. When he was released, so were we.

Next, we were led to another major denomination with a flare for missions. It was great for a season. Then my wife started having dreams. I paid close attention because this was the beginning of her Spirit-filled walk with God. That took a little pressure off of me for a change, too. The pastor at this fellowship got a taste of The Spirit side of life, but the congregation wasn't ready for a drastic swift change. Attendance dropped from the 180s to the low 30s when The Lord finally, once again, released us. Sue's dreams were accurate and she was growing spiritually.

From there we went to a non-denominational fellowship. Coming in the door, one of the first messages we heard delivered to the congregation was concerning willful blindness. I still remember it well, and sadly I watched it played out. I have never looked for a "perfect church". Over the years fellowship has taught me that we are all here to learn, grow, love, be equipped, step into ministry, and then, love even more. The message coming in the door was a real heads-up, and soon it became obvious this house had plenty of opportunities for ministry. Great! Sue and I held a few positions, one of which was mission's directors. I love to travel. I love adventure, but most of all, I love people. Oh, I really do! This was a good fit! But that chump, the devil, has a habit of showing up when things are going well. Two of our mission trips had him as an extra member of our group. When I returned home, I was abruptly called on the carpet by leadership at the accusation of one person, on two separate occasions. It seems I remember a Biblical principle that discourages receiving an accusation from just one person against a leader. But that principle [from 1 Timothy 5:19] got shelved based on another teaching that was held as a higher standard. With the message of being willfully blind, delivered seven years prior, still ringing in my ears, I humbly voiced my stance and bid them adieu.

Why on earth did I bring all of this mess up? Because we have got to grow past business as usual in God's House! It's sad to say that this is my resume in church life. But having been a part of "church" for forty-two years, I've seen more than I've gone through. Usually, things just get swept under the rug until it all dies down, but that doesn't solve a thing. It causes a few others to leave the church with what they perceive to be the problem, and God has to deal with multiple aching hearts while the chump gets a good laugh. Listen, we are all a product of the fall of man, and we all came into this life in need of assistance in the eye department. And guess who is right there to offer us his prescription?

I'd really like to take a break from all this and talk about some more pleasant things. Oh, I know!

CHAPTER 6
WHAT WOULD MOSES DO?

I have to laugh at myself; a lot! I became a follower of Jesus in the last years of the Jesus Movement, and have loved how Jesus shook people up, challenging many things including their trust in Moses. Psalm 90 is such a wonderful picture of a life lived with, for, and in God; a life of peaceful trust and appreciation. Moses writes a request with a "so that". Psalm 90:12 (NASB1995)

"So teach us to number our days,
That we may present to You a heart of wisdom."

The Bible teaches us that God listens when we pray. We can take that to the bank. My life has been described as "interesting" by some people. My Mother used to say, "Don, you've been hard on your body." I'd make a habit of limping home, with yet another broken bone, or gash, but I had fun! There are a few good stories to tell resulting in testimony.

I never concerned myself with "What would Moses do?" until later in life when God called me into intercession. That verse 12 about a heart of wisdom being offered back to God caught my attention. [It actually captured his heart.] After all, with all my experiences, a thing or two had been learned, even if it was the hard way.

I am so glad that recently books and discussions are on the topic of "The Courts of Heaven", but if a person doesn't have a real call to go there it can become just another religious activity. God listens to our heart, and we should be listening to His. If I have any wisdom at all, that is it – Learn to listen to Him. David gave us the structure for these books, and he knew the how and where of the courts. He learned out of necessity. That's right, he fought some battles, and lived an interesting life. This book will be raw and honest, and at times crude to most. Oh, and hopefully totally void of religion.

I like to think I knew about the Courts of Heaven before the books came out, because when they did my heart leaped! The Lord gave me the results I prayed for, and [like David] mine was also out of total need. I never learned all the formalities, but our Father in Heaven didn't seem to be all that concerned with that. He listens to our heart – it speaks louder than any accusation, and humility diffuses them. David demonstrated it all so well.

I prefer to think of the Courts of Heaven as those courtyards in my Father's House where we relax and have real intimate family time.

When attempting to write this, I realized how much of it is my testimony, and I didn't want that. But then The Lord reminded me that this is what He has given me, so I got onboard with Him. There will be a lot of explaining in order to convey the vision. The point is this: the vision, as I understand it, is what God is bringing to us if we want it, and many of us do. But each one [of us] has to choose. Be careful, the enemy doesn't like any of us, and a chump is a chump no matter which suit he puts on, on any given day.

I hope to very candidly bring our modes of operation to the table, and hopefully get rid of them all so we can make room for our Father's Kingdom. We need to be in the mode of ridding ourselves of the spots, blemishes, and wrinkles.

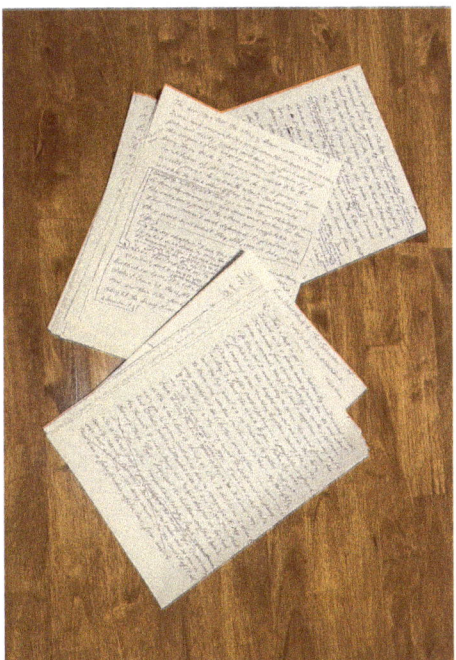

Some of Don's Handwritten Pages for This Book

CHAPTER 7
CLOSURE: BY SUSAN STIVER

This all seems a little sketchy and incomplete when typed from a hand-written manuscript penned by a man whose heart was always after God, and whose thoughts were so deep they were hard to put on paper. Oh, the intimate relationship he had with God, his Father!

Don & Susan

The Lord impressed on me to publish this incomplete labor of love so that God's Story, can be told forever.

Psalm 102:18-21 (The Message)
"Write this down for the next generation
 so people not yet born will praise God.
'God looked out from His high holy place;
 From heaven He surveyed the earth.
He listened to the groans of the doomed,
 He opened the doors of their death cells.'
Write it so the story can be told…"

· · ·

My prayer is that somewhere in this unfinished book you have found some treasure to take away; something that unlocked a question in you that will take you to The Father for deeper revelation.

> It breaks my heart that Don is not here to complete this work.
> He lived life to the hilt, longed for fellowship,
> and dearly loved God and His people!
> You would have loved hearing all of his stories.
> And I can tell you they were amazing, amusing,
> and endless.

> May God stir your heart for fellowship
> and a relationship with Him,
> so that you, too, can tell God's stories,
> and present back to Him
> a heart of wisdom.

ABOUT THE AUTHOR

Don Stiver was, like King David, a man after God's own heart. His passion was to know God, and to make Him known. He met every day with joy and expectancy, waiting to see what God would do, joining Him, then praising Him for His marvelous works and wonders. Always up for a challenge and adventure, he'd find a way to solve any problem, push through the storm, and somehow have fun in the process. His motto was, "You gotta have fun!"

One of his major gifts was his art of storytelling – he had a way of drawing people into the story, teaching history through the story, and sowing seeds to help people think for themselves. He always knew what to say and how to say it using words to edify and encourage people. A true wordsmith.

He was passionate about life and lived it to the fullest – every minute counted, and every person was valued. Not wanting anyone to be lacking or lagging behind, he would engage people in thought-filled conversation, challenging them to think through situations to help them arrive at their own solutions. A word master.

By Bob Jones, he was told that he had a pastor's heart. Through Chris Reed, he was given a word: "You're like a brother to many people who don't have family. It's like that you exhibit and express brotherly love - kinda like the Lord's brother, James." Fellowship was like breathing to him, and he wanted to include everyone in it! He was called a pollinator as he skillfully networked people all through the congregation. It was his gift to the Body.

He loved God and loved people, and true fellowship was the result.

www.ingramcontent.com/pod-product-compliance
Lightning Source LLC
Chambersburg PA
CBHW061742070526
44585CB00024B/2778